V.I. LENIN

Margaret J. Goldstein

Twenty-First Century Books
Minneapolis

For Danny

Note on Dates
Until January 1918, Russia used the Julian, or old style, calendar, which was thirteen days behind the Gregorian calendar used by most countries. The dates mentioned in this book correspond to the particular calendar in official use at the time.

BIOGRAPHY is a trademark of A&E Television Networks. All rights reserved.

Some of the people profiled in this series have also been featured in the acclaimed BIOGRAPHY® series, on The Biography Channel®, which is available on DVD from A&E Home Video. ShopAETV.com.

Twenty-First Century Books
A division of Lerner Publishing Group
241 First Avenue North
Minneapolis, MN 55401 U.S.A.

Website addresses: www.lernerbooks.com
www.biography.com

Library of Congress Cataloging-in-Publication Data

Goldstein, Margaret J.
    Vladimir Lenin / by Margaret J. Goldstein.
        p.   cm. — (Biography)
    Includes bibliographical references and index.
    ISBN-13: 978–0–8225–5977–1 (lib. bdg. : alk. paper)
    ISBN-10: 0–8225–5977–3 (lib. bdg. : alk. paper)
    1. Lenin, Vladimir Ilyich, 1870–1924—Juvenile literature. 2. Heads of state—Soviet Union—Biography—Juvenile literature.
    3. Revolutionaries—Soviet Union—Biography—Juvenile literature.
    I. Title. II. Series: Biography (Twenty-First Century Books (Firm))
    DK254.L455G65   2007
    947.084'1092—dc22 [B]   2006009495

Manufactured in the United States of America
1 2 3 4 5 6 – BP – 12 11 10 09 08 07

CONTENTS

Vladimir Lenin was single minded in his drive to bring revolution to Russia.

INTRODUCTION:
DREAMS OF REVOLUTION

Vladimir Ilyich Lenin was a frustrated man. Forty-six years old in late 1916, he had had only one goal for nearly thirty years. That goal was to bring revolution—the overthrow of the government—to his Russian homeland. Russia was ruled by an all-powerful czar, or emperor. Lenin hoped to inspire Russia's poor and working-class people to rise up against the czar and take over the Russian government for themselves. Then, he believed, revolution would spread from Russia to the whole world.

For nearly three decades, Lenin had worked nonstop: writing about revolution, lecturing about revolution, and scheming with other revolutionaries. He had been arrested and imprisoned for his activities. He had traveled from country to country, running from the police. He had sneaked across borders, written letters in invisible ink, forged papers, and faked his identity. "There's no such person [but Lenin] who is so preoccupied twenty-four hours a day with revolution, who thinks no other thoughts except those about revolution and who even dreams in his sleep about revolution," remarked Fëdor Dan, another Russian revolutionary.

But by 1916, Lenin had grown discouraged. He was nearly out of money. His revolutionary organization, the Bolsheviks, was losing strength. He and his wife, Nadezhda Krupskaya, were by then living in Zurich, Switzerland, far from Russia and out of touch with many of their fellow revolutionaries. Inside Russia, the revolutionary movement was fractured, with various groups fighting with one another. Adding to the uncertainty and instability, almost all of Europe, including Russia, was engulfed in World War I (1914–1918).

Lenin was downhearted. After so many years of work, he was resigned to the fact that revolution might not come in his lifetime. In late January 1917, he addressed a group of young revolutionaries in Zurich. "We of the older generation may not live to see the decisive battles of this coming revolution," he stated.

A few weeks later, Lenin and his wife were home at their apartment in Zurich. Nadezhda was washing the lunch dishes. Lenin was about to go to the library. Suddenly, a young revolutionary named Moisei Bronsky came bounding up the stairs to their apartment, breathless. "Haven't you heard the news?" he cried. "There is revolution in Russia!"

Lenin and his wife were excited but skeptical. They had heard about recent protests and strikes (work stoppages) in Russia. They knew that many Russians were unhappy with the czar, Nicholas II. But Russians had protested many times in the past, and their actions had not led to revolution. The couple was hesitant to believe that revolution had finally come.

Still, the Lenins rushed outside to find a newspaper. To their delight, the story was true. In Petrograd (present-day Saint Petersburg), the Russian capital, a crowd of female factory workers had taken to the streets. Because of the war, the city was suffering from drastic food shortages. The women demanded bread and peace. The next day, thousands more joined in the protest. Soon, hundreds of thousands of people filled the streets of Petrograd. They carried banners and shouted slogans, denouncing Czar Nicholas and demanding an end to the war. A few days later, masses of soldiers joined the demonstration. They refused to follow orders from their commanders. They attacked the czar's palace, stormed police headquarters, and stole thousands of weapons from government storehouses.

Czar Nicholas was away from Petrograd when the revolution occurred. But he knew that he had lost his authority and the respect of his people. On March 2, 1917, he gave up his throne.

Reading about the events in the Swiss newspapers, Vladimir Lenin was thrilled. The revolution had finally arrived. But it needed a leader, and Lenin was convinced that he—and only he—was the person to steer Russia through this crucial point in its history. His mind was racing. He had to get to Russia immediately.

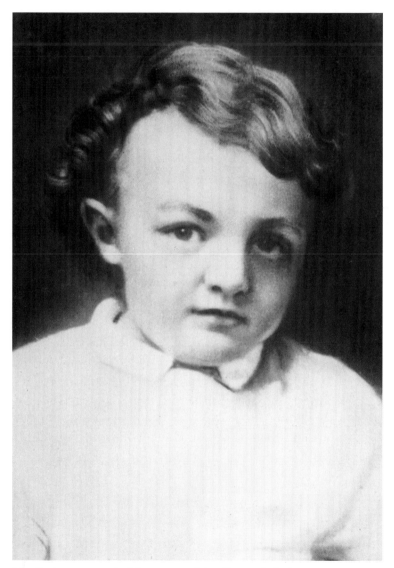

Vladimir was a mischievous and intelligent little boy.

Chapter **ONE**

A LIFE OF EASY CIRCUMSTANCES

WE LIVED IN EASY CIRCUMSTANCES," RECALLED AN adult Vladimir Lenin, reflecting on his childhood. "We did not know hunger or cold; we were surrounded by all sorts of cultural opportunities and stimuli, books, music, and diversions." That childhood took place in the town of Simbirsk, Russia, where Vladimir Lenin was born on April 10, 1870. But Lenin was not his original last name. His name at birth was Vladimir Ilyich Ulyanov.

With about thirty thousand residents, Simbirsk was a quiet town on the Volga River. It was located in the Russian heartland, far from the thriving city of Moscow and even farther from Saint Petersburg (as Petrograd was called at the time).

Simbirsk perched on a hill above the Volga. Nobles—people of wealth, status, and power—made their homes at the top of the hill, in a neighborhood called the Crown. It was filled with stately houses, wide streets, and government offices. The middle classes—merchants, schoolteachers, and other professionals—lived farther down the hill. Working-class people lived on the edges of town, where they crowded into ramshackle wooden houses on narrow and muddy streets. Peasants, or farming people, lived in the countryside beyond town. Many of them were desperately poor.

The Ulyanovs belonged to the ranks of the town's middle classes. When Vladimir was born, his father, Ilya Nikolaevich Ulyanov, worked for the government as a school inspector. Vladimir's mother, Maria Alexanderovna Ulyanov, was the daughter of a well-off doctor. The family lived on Streletsky Street, near the Crown, in part of a two-story wooden house, which they rented from another family. Vladimir was the third child born to Ilya and Maria. Eventually, the Ulyanov family had six children, named, from oldest to youngest, Anna, Alexander, Vladimir, Olga, Dmitri, and Maria.

The children enjoyed a pleasant childhood. They loved games such as hide-and-seek, blindman's bluff, and croquet in summer. They went ice-skating and sledding in winter. Every summer, Maria would take the children to vacation at her father's fancy estate in

Kokushkino, near the town of Kazan. They traveled there by steamboat, sailing up the Volga. At Kokushkino, more pleasures awaited the children: boating, swimming, and hunting in the nearby woods.

FORWARD PROGRESS

Vladimir's father, Ilya, was often away on business. He was a dedicated government worker, employed by the Ministry of Education. A churchgoing and patriotic Russian, Ilya was loyal to the Russian czar, Alexander II.

The czar was an autocrat—a ruler with absolute power. According to Russian beliefs, he ruled with God's permission. He did not share authority with a parliament (legislature) or other elected officials. His word was law. At the time, Russian citizens did not have the right to vote. They had no freedom of speech or freedom of the press. The czar's secret police kept a close watch on suspected troublemakers, and government censors reviewed publications to make sure that writers did not stir up opposition to the czar.

Despite these restrictions, Ilya Ulyanov thought Alexander II was a fair and good leader. He had passed a series of reforms intended to improve the lives of Russian people. One law gave peasants more freedom and the opportunity to own collective (shared) farms. Another law created local governing councils, which gave citizens some say in the running of their towns and villages. Ilya supported these reforms and thought that more would soon follow. He saw new industries opening in big cities. He saw new technologies such as railroads and telegraph systems improving people's lives. It seemed to Ilya that Russia was steadily becoming a modern, enlightened nation.

Both Ilya and Maria Ulyanov were interested in new ideas. They closely followed the work of western European artists, musicians, scientists, and philosophers. Maria hadn't had a formal education. But she had been tutored at home by an aunt, who taught her several languages. In addition to Russian, she spoke English, German, and French. Naturally, the Ulyanovs wanted the best education for their own children. After their last son, Dmitri, was born in 1874, they hired a tutor to prepare the children for formal schooling.

The Little Barrel

As a young boy, Vladimir Ulyanov was short and stocky, with curly reddish-brown hair and hazel eyes. Because of his stout build, his family gave him a nickname, Kubyshka, which means "little barrel." Vladimir could be bossy, loud, and mischievous. He liked to break his toys and tease his younger brother and sisters. Of all his siblings, Vladimir was closest to his sister Olga, who was one year younger. They sang and played together. When Vladimir was five and Olga was four, their mother taught them both to read. Then Vladimir began his studies with the family tutor.

In 1878 Ilya earned a promotion. He became the director of public schools for Simbirsk Province. This position marked an important step up for Ilya. With his promotion, he achieved the rank of nobleman in the Russian government. The rank came with a high title, His Excellency.

That same year, the family bought their own house, located at 48 Moscow Street, farther up the hill toward the Crown. The move represented another step up for the Ulyanovs, who were growing ever more wealthy.

The Ulyanov family in 1879. Dmitri and Vladimir (far right) *sit in front. Behind them, from left to right, are Olga, Maria (with baby Maria on her lap), Alexander, Ilya, and Anna.*

Rich and Poor

Russia in the late nineteenth century was a land of great contrast between rich and poor. A small minority of Russians prospered in czarist Russia. Industrialists—people who owned big businesses such as factories, mines, and railroads—reaped great profits from their ventures. Nobles, most of whom had inherited wealth and land from their ancestors, enjoyed lives of ease and pleasure on great country estates.

But the vast majority of Russians suffered under the czarist system. In the cities, factory workers toiled six days a week, twelve hours a day, under brutal and dangerous conditions. Their wages were barely enough for survival. In the countryside, peasants performed backbreaking farm labor. Some were so poor that they had to pull plows themselves because they could not afford animals to pull them. Most peasants lived in run-down homes made of wood or clay. If the crops failed, people went hungry and sometimes even starved to death.

At age nine, Vladimir was ready for formal schooling. His tutor had prepared him well. He easily passed the difficult admission tests and entered Simbirsk Classical Gimnazia, where his older brother, Alexander, was already a student. Their older sister, Anna, attended the Simbirsk Marinskaya Gimnazia, a similar school for girls. Priests ran the schools.

Vladimir's class was made up of thirty boys. Each

student wore a uniform, including a dark blue tunic with nine brass buttons and an upturned collar Vladimir quickly excelled in the classroom, earning top marks in handwriting, Russian, math, and science.

PEOPLE'S WILL

On March 1, 1881, when Vladimir was ten years old, a dramatic event rocked Russia. Bombers set off two explosions near Czar Alexander's carriage outside his palace in Saint Petersburg. The second explosion killed the czar.

The bombers belonged to a radical group called People's Will. Its goal was to topple the entire Russian political system and replace it with a more fair and just government. People's Will believed that once the

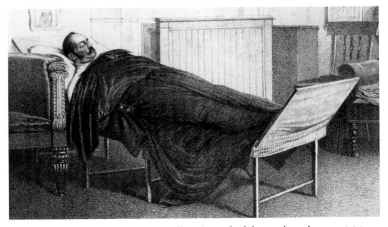

Czar Alexander II was mortally wounded by a bomb in 1881. This drawing depicts the czar on his deathbed.

czar was dead, poor people would rise up in a revolution and take control of Russia's government for themselves.

But People's Will had misread the mood of ordinary Russians. Alexander's death did not lead to a popular uprising as the group had hoped. People such as the Ulyanovs—God-fearing, law-abiding citizens who had faith in the czar and the Russian system—were distressed by the assassination. In Simbirsk, Vladimir and his family attended a memorial service for the czar at the town cathedral. At Vladimir's school, a priest described the revolutionaries as "outcasts of the human race." The assassination backfired in another way. The murdered czar was replaced by his son, Alexander III, who proved be an even tougher autocrat than his father.

THE YOUNG SCHOLAR

No revolution happened, and life continued as normal for the Ulyanov family. First Anna and then Alexander graduated from their schools and moved to Saint Petersburg to attend college. Vladimir continued to excel at school. He earned the top mark—a five out of five—in Greek, Latin, German, algebra, and other classes. He once scored even higher—a five-plus—in composition, or writing, class. When writing an essay, Vladimir always began with a thorough outline. He impressed his teachers with his well-crafted sentences and convincing arguments.

Vladimir's favorite classes were history and literature. He loved the works of great Russian novelists
such as Nikolay Gogol, Leo Tolstoy, and Ivan Tur-
genev. After school, Vladimir finished his homework
so quickly that his father wondered if the boy was
cutting corners. But when Ilya quizzed his son on his
lessons, Vladimir showed that he had mastered them
perfectly.

But socially, Vladimir did not excel. He had no close
friends at school. His schoolmates remembered him
as a loner. He was very self-confident and could also
be rude and condescending. His unfriendliness and
attitude of superiority distanced him from his fellow
students. But everyone agreed—teachers, parents, and
classmates—that Vladimir Ulyanov was headed toward
a bright future. It appeared that nothing would stand
in the way of his success.

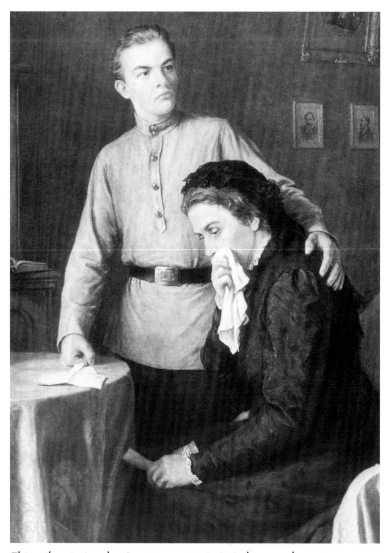

This oil painting by Russian artist P. P. Belousov shows teenage
Vladimir comforting his mother following his father's death.

Chapter **TWO**

A SUDDEN ADULT

THE YEAR **1886** BEGAN DARKLY FOR THE **U**LYANOV family. Less than two weeks into the new year, on January 12, fifty-three-year-old Ilya Ulyanov died suddenly of a brain hemorrhage. The family was grief stricken. Vladimir, not yet sixteen, was the chief pallbearer at his father's funeral.

The family had lost its main breadwinner. But Maria still had several sources of income. The government gave her a generous pension, or regular payment, based on her husband's long service with the Ministry of Education. She had also inherited a portion of her father's estate in Kazan and earned money by renting out some of the land there to farmers. Finally, she moved her family into one-half of their house on Moscow Street and rented out the other half.

The children continued their schooling. Alexander was by then in his fourth year at Saint Petersburg University. He specialized in the sciences. Anna also attended college in Saint Petersburg, where she was studying to be a teacher. Vladimir remained at home with his mother and younger siblings. Outwardly, he did not show much emotion at his father's death. Already a loner, he withdrew even more into his books, especially Russian novels. He also stopped going to church, claiming that he no longer believed in God.

A Tragic Turn

Alexander Ulyanov excelled at Saint Petersburg University just as he had at the Simbirsk Gimnazia. Everyone in the family expected him to become a science professor. But Alexander was keeping an important part of his life hidden from his family. Along with studying zoology and chemistry, he secretly read the works of radical thinkers such as the Germans Karl Marx and Friedrich Engels and Russia's Georgy Plekhanov. These philosophers examined the workings of capitalism—or private business ownership. They wrote about how business owners, labeled the bourgeoisie, took advantage of workers, called the proletariat. Marx, Engels, and Plekhanov believed that capitalism would eventually fail and be replaced by socialism, a system in which everyone owned land and businesses in common and shared in society's wealth equally.

Alexander studied these ideas and discussed them with fellow students. As he did, he became more and more angry with the Russian system of government— a system that allowed a small group of people to live lives of ease, while millions of working-class people endured terrible poverty. Alexander became convinced that Russia's government needed to change. Late in 1886, he joined a group of radical students modeling themselves on People's Will.

Like other radicals before them, Alexander and his colleagues decided that the only way to bring about change in their nation was to kill the czar. That deed, they believed, would lead the way for working people to form a socialist society. The young people collected guns and ingredients for building bombs. Alexander Ulyanov, the gifted scientist, was put in charge of the bomb making.

But the czar's secret police force, the Okhrana, knew that universities were a hotbed of radicalism. It kept a close watch on certain students, reading their mail and secretly following them. On March 1, 1887, the police stopped five suspicious students on the Nevsky Prospect, the main street in Saint Petersburg. Concealed among their books and clothing were pistols and bombs intended to help them kill the czar. The police arrested the five students and rounded up their coconspirators, including Alexander Ulyanov. The police also arrested Anna Ulyanov, although she had had no knowledge of her brother's plot.

When word arrived that her children had been arrested, Maria Ulyanov rushed to Saint Petersburg. She sent a letter to the czar himself, pleading for her son's life. At the trial, held from March 15 to March 19, Alexander refused to express remorse or beg for mercy as some of his coconspirators had done. In fact, he used the occasion of his trial to further criticize the czarist system. The results were grim. While some of the defendants received long prison terms, Alexander and four others were sentenced to hang. That punishment was carried out on May 8.

Several days after her brother's execution, Anna Ulyanov was released from prison. She had been found innocent of plotting against the czar. Nevertheless, the authorities sentenced her to house arrest at Kokushkino, her mother's estate, where she would be under police watch.

In Simbirsk, the family was grief stricken once more. But Vladimir, in his last year at the gimnazium, kept his emotions in check. He methodically completed his final examinations, which took place throughout the month of May, including on the day of his brother's hanging. Still, Vladimir was clearly shaken by Alexander's death. According to one teacher, "He ceased to joke, rarely smiled, and somehow all of a sudden became an adult." Compounding the

Ulyanovs' misery, the whole town shunned them that spring. No one wanted to be associated with the family of a convicted terrorist.

STARTING OVER

Vladimir graduated from Simbirsk Classical Gimnazia with a gold medal, an honor given to the top student in each class. He had hoped to attend Saint Petersburg University as Alexander had done, but his brother's crime barred him from admission. Instead, he applied to the law school at Imperial Kazan University, his father's alma mater, in the town of Kazan. His headmaster at the Simbirsk Gimnazia wrote him a glowing recommendation.

Imperial Kazan University accepted the promising young law student. But knowing that Vladimir was the brother of the executed terrorist Alexander Ulyanov, university officials kept a close eye on him. Maria Ulyanov intended to keep an eye on her son too. She decided to sell the family home and move everyone to Kazan, where she could be sure that Vladimir stayed out of trouble.

As always, the family spent the summer at Kokushkino, where Vladimir read a novel called *What Is to Be Done?* by Russian writer Nikolay Chernyshevsky. The novel describes how a group of tireless and idealistic young people turn their nation into a socialist paradise, in which everyone enjoys a life of ease. The book captivated Vladimir, who read it five times that summer.

His Brother's Path

Seventeen-year-old Vladimir began law school at Imperial Kazan University in the fall of 1887. But early in the term, his schooling came to an abrupt end. On December 4, he joined several hundred other students in a protest against some harsh university regulations. Later that night, the police rounded up those thought to be ringleaders of the protest, including freshman Vladimir Ulyanov. In fact, Vladimir had not been among the organizers but had merely attended the event. But the police and university officials were quick to condemn him as Alexander Ulyanov's brother. Along with thirty-nine others, he was expelled from school and banished from Kazan.

Maria convinced the authorities to allow Vladimir to live at Kokushkino, where his sister Anna was already living under police watch. So Vladimir joined his sister at the comfortable family estate. He passed the winter devouring books.

In May 1888, Vladimir made a formal request to the minister of education for readmission to Imperial Kazan University. But officials had already pegged Vladimir as a potential terrorist. "Isn't this the brother of *that* Ulyanov?" the minister of education wrote on Vladimir's paperwork. "He should certainly not be admitted."

In September Vladimir made another request for readmission and was again turned down. But he was allowed to return to live with his family in Kazan. There, he continued his tireless reading, this time discovering the works of Karl Marx, which his brother had studied before him. Marx's *Das Kapital* (Capital) enthralled Vladimir. The book explained the workings of capitalism and how, inevitably, capitalism would fail and be replaced by communism, an extreme form of socialism.

Maria Ulyanov was determined to keep her second son from following in his big brother's revolutionary footsteps. With money from the sale of her home, she bought a 225-acre (91-hectare) farm thirty miles (48 kilometers) east of the town of Samara. She moved the family there. In this out-of-the-way place, she hoped, eighteen-year-old Vladimir would manage the farm and forget all thoughts of politics.

Vladimir halfheartedly agreed to his mother's plan, but he quickly abandoned it. Instead, he hired a professional manager to run the farm for him. Then, setting up a bench and table in the garden of the farmhouse, he settled in with his books by Marx and others. He read for hours on end, taking pages and pages of notes.

In the winter of 1888–1889, realizing that her son had not found his calling as a farmer, Maria packed up her family once more and moved them to Samara. Vladimir met the town's other revolutionaries, some of whom were affiliated with People's Will. They gathered secretly, discussing the works of Marx and how Marx's ideas might be applied to the political and economic problems facing Russia. Although educated and generally well off, these activists despised the upper

ANALYZING ULYANOV

ike his fellow Marxists, Vladimir Ulyanov hated the czar and the upper classes. He attacked the Russian nobility as "irresponsible, corrupt, savage, ignorant, and parasitic [living off the labor of the poor]." But his attitude was somewhat puzzling. After all, he himself was a nobleman, with a title inherited from his father. Examining Lenin many years after his death, most scholars believe that his deep hatred of the czar and nobility stemmed from his brother's execution and the subsequent shunning of his family by the upper-class townspeople in Simbirsk.

classes and the czar. They wanted to change the world for the benefit of poor working people.

A CRASH COURSE IN LAW

Vladimir hadn't given up his thoughts of becoming a lawyer. He wrote the minister of education again, this time asking if he could take the final law school exams at a university, even though he wasn't enrolled as a student. After his request was denied, his mother followed up with the same request. In June 1890, the minister finally agreed that Vladimir could take the law exams at Saint Petersburg University.

With his usual zeal, Vladimir set about teaching himself the law through books. For more than a year, he studied day after day. In November 1891, he took a

At age twenty-one, Lenin was already gruff and serious. Within two years, colleagues nicknamed him the Old Man.

long series of law tests at Saint Petersburg University. Much to the dismay of the law school examiners, the almost entirely self-taught young man passed first out of a class of 124 students.

With his diploma in hand, Vladimir returned to Samara to begin a law practice. But despite all his preparation, Vladimir didn't prosper as a lawyer. He took a handful of cases, defending peasants and workers accused of minor crimes, and lost all of them. His real passion was revolution—the day the workers would rise up against the czar and the upper classes.

If the revolution were going to happen, Vladimir believed, it wasn't going to occur in a small no-name town like Samara. He wanted to be where the action was, in a big city with great masses of industrial workers—the proletariat. So in the summer of 1893, Vladimir moved to Saint Petersburg.

In the late nineteenth century, Saint Petersburg was home to many university students, intellectuals, and political activists.

Chapter **THREE**

PROFESSIONAL REVOLUTIONARY

VLADIMIR ILYICH ULYANOV ARRIVED IN SAINT
Petersburg at age twenty-three. But he looked much
older. He had started to go bald. He had narrow eyes,
deep lines on his face, a thin reddish beard and
mustache, stooped shoulders, and a harsh voice.
Colleagues noted that he also acted much older than a
man in his early twenties. According to one acquain-
tance, Ulyanov appeared to be a "politically fully
formed and mature person." Another added, "Vladimir
Ilyich already seemed a man whose views were
completely formed, and who conducted himself at
group gatherings ... with assurance and complete
independence." Fellow revolutionaries took to calling
him Starik, meaning the "old man."

Ulyanov rented a room in a boardinghouse on Kazachy Street and found a job as an assistant to a Saint Petersburg lawyer. But his real work was revolution. He joined other Saint Petersburg intellectuals at meetings called discussion circles. There, they examined revolutionary writings, debated one another, and made plans for revolution. Concealing their identities with fake names, they snuck into factories and working-class neighborhoods, asking questions about working conditions and lecturing workers about Marxism and other revolutionary ideas. Since the Okhrana kept a close watch on suspected revolutionaries, such activities took place in secret.

Ulyanov quickly became a leader in the city's revolutionary community. At discussion circles, he overwhelmed his fellow revolutionaries with "a torrent [flood] of statistics which he used to illustrate his points." He was a powerful speaker, with a masterful command of history, economics, and political science. Many colleagues were drawn to his boldness and self-confidence. But others were put off. "Truly, in his attitude to his fellow men, Lenin breathed coldness, contempt, and cruelty," remarked Pyotr Struve, a fellow Marxist.

Ulyanov and the other Saint Petersburg revolutionaries disagreed on how a change in Russia's government would take place. According to the teachings of Marx, society moved naturally through economic stages—advancing from a rural, agricultural economy to a capitalist, industrial economy, and then finally to communism.

KARL MARX
AND THE COMMUNIST IDEAL

Many economists and philosophers wrote about socialism in the nineteenth century. But none was more influential than Karl Marx. Marx was born in Germany in 1818. As a university student, he studied law and philosophy. He worked as a journalist in Cologne, Germany, and later moved to Paris, France, where he formed many of his economic ideas.

Marx studied capitalism, or private business ownership. Under capitalism, he observed, a small group of business owners grew rich while the great mass of workers were underpaid for their labors. Under the capitalist system, he predicted, wealth would become concentrated in the hands of fewer and fewer people, the economy would suffer periodic depressions, and working people would grow increasingly poor. Finally, workers would revolt and seize control of industry and government for themselves. Marx believed workers would then establish communism—a form of socialism—with state control of all land, factories, and other economic resources.

Marx described his ideas in two famous books. In *The Communist Manifesto*, written with German economist Friedrich Engels in 1848, he discussed the flaws of capitalism and predicted its collapse. The book also promoted communism as an ideal economic system, one in which everyone would share equally in society's wealth. Marx and Engels urged the proletariat to join an international workers' association. "Let the ruling class tremble at the communist revolution," they wrote. "The proletarians have nothing to lose but their chains. They have a world to win. Workers of all countries, unite." In *Das Kapital* (Capital), published in three volumes between 1867 and 1894 and completed by Engels after Marx's death, Marx examined the underlying economic theory behind capitalism and the process by which capitalism would be replaced by communism.

Some of the Saint Petersburg revolutionaries, called the Narodniks, or populists, thought Russia would skip the capitalist stage altogether. They believed that poor, farming people would rise up in revolution and lead Russia straight from an agrarian (farming) economy to communism. Other revolutionaries disagreed. They thought Russia was in the early stages of capitalism. Over time, they believed, the capitalist system would grow, inevitably fail, and then give way to communism. Vladimir Ulyanov was less patient than his colleagues. He argued that Russia already had an advanced capitalist economy. Therefore, he argued, the time for revolution was at hand.

KINDRED SPIRITS

To many observers, Vladimir Ulyanov seemed to have only one true love: revolution. He showed little interest in women or dating. But occasionally, a woman caught his attention. One was Nadezhda Krupskaya, whom he met at a Marxist discussion circle in February 1894. A tall, serious young woman, one year older than Ulyanov, Krupskaya shared his commitment to revolution. She was a no-nonsense revolutionary who always dressed in black and wore her long hair pulled tightly behind her head. Ulyanov called her Nadya. The two became close companions.

In May 1895, the Saint Petersburg Marxists gave Ulyanov an exciting assignment. They wanted to

Nadezhda Krupskaya was a dedicated Marxist.

strengthen ties with the Emancipation of Labor Group, a Marxist organization with cells, or units, throughout western Europe. They sent Ulyanov on a four-month trip to Austria, Switzerland, France, and Germany to make contact with Emancipation of Labor allies. Traveling by train, Ulyanov first arrived in Geneva, Switzerland, where he met with Georgy Plekhanov, considered the godfather of Russian Marxism. In Paris Ulyanov met with Paul Lafargue, the son-in-law of the deceased Karl Marx. He also gave lectures and speeches and met with Marxists in other cities before returning to Saint Petersburg in September 1895. He brought back volumes of illegal Marxist literature, hidden inside the false bottom of his trunk.

No Compromise

Marxists weren't the only ones who wanted to change Russia at this time. Many Russians—rich and poor— were unhappy with their government. They resented the almighty czar who denied Russians a voice in their own government. (A new czar, Nicholas II, had inherited the Russian throne in 1894.) Some Russians hoped their nation would become a democracy, similar to the United States or the nations of western Europe. They did not want to overthrow Nicholas altogether. Instead they hoped he would share power with a parliament, a group of lawmakers elected by the people. They also hoped Nicholas would draft a constitution, a document that laid out the rights of

Czar Nicholas II

Russian citizens and the rules of law. Liberal-minded Russians believed that reform, not revolution, was the key to Russia's future. To improve workers' lives, many liberals supported the creation of trade unions—groups of workers that would fight for safer working conditions, a shorter workday, and higher pay. These Russians thought their nation could be improved legally, by working within the established government system, without violence or bloodshed.

Ulyanov would have none of such ideas. He saw liberals and reformers as members of the bourgeoisie and enemies of the proletariat. He thought their ideas would do nothing to fundamentally change Russian society or the corrupt capitalist system. Ulyanov had made up his mind that only communism—"dictatorship of the proletariat" in the words of Marx—would bring justice, equality, and harmony to humankind. Ulyanov, like Marx, did not object to violence, if it were necessary to bring down the existing government. Ulyanov verbally attacked other Marxists who even considered the idea of compromising with the czar. He was a by-the-book Marxist. He and others who faithfully followed Marx's teaching called themselves Social Democrats.

EXILE

The Saint Petersburg Marxists continued their illegal work. They wrote documents using invisible ink and secret codes. But the Okhrana was on their trail. Disguised as a Marxist, one of its agents attended their secret meetings. On December 9, 1895, the police caught Ulyanov and several colleagues in the process of creating an illegal newspaper. They were arrested and sent to the House of Preliminary Detention in Saint Petersburg.

As he awaited sentencing, Ulyanov's imprisonment dragged on for more than a year. He lived alone in cell 193. The cell was cold, but he suffered little. The authorities allowed his family to send him books, money, food, and other supplies. He spent his days reading and writing a book of his own, *The Development of Capitalism in Russia*. He wrote and received letters in invisible ink. (Dropping the paper into the hot water he used to make tea made the words visible.) In fact, it seemed that Ulyanov actually enjoyed his stay in prison. It gave him nothing but free time to read and write. He joked that if had been allowed to stay behind bars a little longer, he could have finished his book.

In January 1897, Ulyanov finally received his punishment for his revolutionary activities: three years in exile in Siberia. At the time, exile to Siberia—a vast, bitterly cold, barren region of central and eastern Russia—was a common punishment. Exiles were not imprisoned but simply lived in remote Siberian villages under police oversight. There, far from big cities, the authorities believed the exiles could not work against the government or otherwise stir up trouble.

Ulyanov was exiled to Shushenskoye, a town of just fifteen hundred inhabitants on the Shush River. He rented a room in a peasant's hut and settled in to pursue his usual pastimes: writing, reading, hunting in the nearby woods, swimming, and ice-skating. His family kept him well supplied with necessities, including gloves, warm clothing, books, newspapers, pencils, and ammunition for his hunting rifle. Ulyanov also kept up with news from Saint Petersburg and other big cities. He learned that in March of 1898, a small group of fellow Social Democrats had held the First Congress of the Russian Social Democratic Labor Party (RSDLP)—the first formal meeting of Social Democrats—in the Russian city of Minsk.

This painting shows Ulyanov speaking with villagers in Siberia. Many creative works exaggerated or distorted the details of his life.

Around the same time, Ulyanov's companion, Nadya Krupskaya, was arrested at a meeting of revolutionaries in Saint Petersburg. She was sentenced to exile in Ufa, in the western part of Siberia. Claiming they were engaged, Krupskaya and Ulyanov requested that she be allowed to join him and marry him in Shushenskoye. The request was granted. In the spring of 1898, Krupskaya arrived, accompanied by her mother. (It was not uncommon then for family members to live with their relatives in exile.) On July 10, 1898, a local priest, Father Orest, married the couple at the Peter-Paul Church. They exchanged wedding rings fashioned out of pieces of copper coins.

In exile, the newlyweds continued their revolutionary work. Ulyanov wrote an article called *The Tasks of the Russian Social Democrats*. In it, he explained why only the proletariat were suited to carry out revolution. Factory workers, he wrote, "are . . . the most important by virtue of their numbers and concentration in the nation's political centers." Peasants were too backward, uneducated, and disorganized to be revolutionaries, he said. And intellectuals (his own group) were likely to sell out to the bourgeoisie for "an official salary or a share of the profits." He concluded that "The proletariat alone can be the frontline fighters for political liberty."

With Krupskaya's editorial assistance, Ulyanov also continued writing *The Development of Capitalism in Russia*. He finished the work in the summer of 1898 and made arrangements for a Saint Petersburg publisher to print twenty-four hundred copies. Published under the named Vladimir Ilin to disguise its author's identity, the work argued that since Russia was already a well-developed capitalist country, it was time first to take apart the czarist monarchy and second to create a socialist revolution.

Ulyanov's exile ended on January 29, 1900, but Krupskaya still had a year left on her sentence, which she had to carry out in Ufa. With five hundred pounds of books loaded into a carriage, the couple and Krupskaya's mother left Shushenskoye on February 10. They headed first to Ufa, where Ulyanov said goodbye to his wife and mother-in-law. Then he went back to the west of Russia, determined to take revolution to the next level.

Ulyanov in 1900, after his return from exile.

Chapter **FOUR**

THE SPARK

BACK IN WESTERN RUSSIA, VLADIMIR ULYANOV
had a plan. Along with other Social Democrats,
he wanted to print a newspaper to spread the
message of the newly formed RSDLP. Since printing
a revolutionary paper under the nose of the
Okhrana was too risky, Ulyanov and his colleagues
decided to produce the paper abroad and have
it smuggled into Russia. They would call the
paper *Iskra* (Spark), a name taken from an old
revolutionary saying, "A spark will start a big
blaze." *Iskra*, Ulyanov believed, would ignite
the flame of revolution in Russia. He was also
convinced that revolution in Russia would set off
revolution worldwide.

Ulyanov spent a few months in western Russia, visiting friends and family. Then he traveled by train to Switzerland, where he met once again with Georgy Plekhanov, the great Marxist thinker. Along with four other revolutionaries, they formed an editorial board to guide *Iskra*. The group also decided to publish a revolutionary magazine called *Zarya* (Dawn). They secured funding from wealthy Russians and others who were sympathetic to the revolutionary cause.

The editors chose Munich, Germany, as the safest place to produce the publications. Plekhanov remained in Switzerland, but the other board members went to Munich and made arrangements with a typesetter and a printer. The first issue of *Iskra* appeared in December 1900. By then, Nadya Krupskaya had been released from exile. She joined her husband in Munich.

"VANGUARD OF THE PROLETARIAT"

Along with *Iskra* and *Zarya*, Ulyanov also worked on a new book. Taking the title from the Chernyshevsky novel that had so influenced him as a young man, he named the work *What Is to Be Done?* The book mapped out Ulyanov's revolutionary philosophy, one that distinguished him from the majority of other Marxists—and from Karl Marx himself.

Marx had predicted that workers would rise up in revolution spontaneously and that they, themselves, would lead the revolution. In *What Is to Be Done?*

Ulyanov argued that revolution would succeed only if a small, highly trained group of revolutionaries led the movement. He said that on their own, industrial workers would never become revolutionaries. They would simply become trade unionists, willing to bargain and compromise with their employers for limited gains. To successfully create a communist society, Ulyanov said, the workers needed full-time, professional revolutionaries to guide them. "It is necessary to prepare men who devote to the revolution not only their free evenings, but their entire lives," he wrote. And he promised, "Give us an organization of revolutionaries, and we will overturn Russia."

Ulyanov described such revolutionaries vividly. He said they would work in secret. They would be spies inside the government, the church, the police, the courts, the nobility, and every other institution of Russian society. They would use terror, if necessary, to achieve their goals. And their revolutionary party would not be democratic, with rank-and-file members having a say in its running. Instead, a very small group—preferably one man—would make all the decisions for the organization.

What Is to Be Done? came out in March 1902. Some readers were shocked by its radical departure from traditional Marxist teachings. Others loved the book.

Vladimir Ulyanov did not publish the book under his real name. Over the years, in the process of hiding from the authorities, he had employed many pseudonyms, or false names: Petrov, Tulin, Ilin, Ivanov, Richter, Meyer, and many others. This time, he chose the pseudonym N. Lenin—an alias he had used only once before. When *What Is to Be Done?* became famous, the name Lenin became famous too. And Lenin's interpretation of Marxism would come to be known as Leninism.

DIVISION

The Munich police were starting to harass the *Iskra* staff, so the editorial board decided it would be safer to produce their newspaper in London, England. London had an active socialist community, and the police rarely bothered them. Lenin and Krupskaya rented a two-room apartment on Holford Square, while the other editors shared a separate apartment nearby.

WHY LENIN?

How did Vladimir Ulyanov come up with the name Lenin? Many historians believe that Lenin derives from Lena, the name of a large Siberian river. The name was just one of more than seventy-five pseudonyms that Ulyanov used in his lifetime. Even after he became famous as Lenin, he continued to use other pseudonyms.

Early one morning in the fall of 1902, Lenin and Krupskaya were awakened by a knock on the door. The caller was a bespectacled young man with a thick head of wavy dark hair. He was Lev Davidovich Bronstein, but he went by the alias Leon Trotsky. Only twenty-two, he was already a dedicated revolutionary who idolized Lenin. He had come to London to join his hero in revolutionary work. Lenin quickly took a liking to Trotsky. He was impressed by the young man's sharp mind and commitment to the revolutionary cause.

In 1903 *Iskra* moved its headquarters again, this time to Geneva, Switzerland, where Plekhanov lived. There, Lenin and his wife rented a small house. That summer the RSDLP held its second congress (conference). The

Like Lenin, Leon Trotsky had been exiled to Siberia. He escaped to join Lenin in London.

meeting started in Brussels, Belgium, but when the Belgian police arrested some of the delegates, the rest of the group moved to London.

At the congress, Lenin insisted that the RSDLP should be a party of disciplined, professional revolutionaries, taking orders from a powerful Central Committee. In contrast, Julius Martov, one of the other *Iskra* editors, argued that the party should be a looser association, whose members were committed to revolution but did not necessarily pursue it full-time. Martov also wanted workers themselves, not an elite Central Committee, to lead the revolution. The congress split into two camps, those backing Lenin and those backing Martov.

Martov's camp was larger than Lenin's, but on one vote, Lenin's group held sway. Lenin took advantage of this situation to declare his supporters to be the Bolsheviks, which means "majorityites" in Russian. Martov called his group the Mensheviks, or "minorityites." The names were inaccurate, since the Mensheviks, not the Bolsheviks, held a majority in the party. But the name Bolshevik no doubt gave Lenin's group an aura of weight and power.

Most of Lenin's colleagues, including Leon Trotsky, sided with the Mensheviks. They were disturbed by Lenin's notion of an iron-fisted Central Committee, which Trotsky called "a dictatorship over the proletariat," instead of a dictatorship of the proletariat. Many worried that Lenin was simply trying to make himself a dictator. In December 1903, Lenin resigned from the *Iskra* editorial board. He attacked Plekhanov, Martov, and others in person and in print.

But Lenin still had followers. Many of them were fans of *What Is to Be Done?* Others were attracted to his nerve and confidence as much as to his ideas. One fellow revolutionary explained that Lenin had a hypnotic effect on those who met him. Lenin continued to draw followers even as his politics became more extreme. Seeking funds from backers throughout Europe, he planned a new newspaper, *Vperyod* (Forward), to promote the Bolshevik message. (Lenin also routinely received money from his mother, which he used to support himself and his wife.)

1905

Back in Russia, people were unhappier than ever with the czarist government, and they were starting to demand changes. The peasants wanted changes to land laws that kept them at the edge of starvation. Industrial workers wanted reforms such as a guaranteed minimum wage and safer working conditions. And Russians of every class wanted democratic reforms such as a parliament, a constitution, freedom of speech, and freedom of the press. Further angering Russians, their nation went to war with Japan and then suffered humiliating defeats both on land and at sea. Russians started to doubt the czar's ability to rule and to protect them.

In some places, workers went on strike, or refused to work. In the countryside, peasants set fire to landowners' homes and seized land from nobles. Students demonstrated. A group called the Social Revolutionaries (SRs), an offshoot of the Narodniks, assassinated several government ministers. Russia was alive with unrest. The discontent came to a head on Sunday, January 9, 1905. On that day, Georgy Gapon, a Russian Orthodox priest, led a mass of men, women, and children—some two hundred thousand in all—through the streets of Saint Petersburg. Most of the adult marchers were striking factory workers. They headed to the czar's Winter Palace, carrying a petition addressed to Czar Nicholas. With more than 135,000 signatures, the petition contained a list of demands, including an eight-hour workday, universal education, and an end to the Russo-Japanese War. In part, the petition read:

> We are become beggars, bowing under oppression and burdened by toil beyond our powers, scorned, no longer regarded as human beings, treated as slaves who must suffer their bitter lot in silence. And having suffered, we are driven deeper and deeper into the abyss of poverty, lawlessness, and ignorance. . . . We have abandoned our work and declared to our masters that we shall not begin to work again until they comply with our demands.

The petition was never delivered. Before the demonstrators reached the Winter Palace, soldiers fired upon the crowd, killing hundreds. The procession scattered. As word of "Bloody Sunday" spread, additional uprisings and demonstrations erupted across Russia.

When news of the event reached Geneva, Lenin was thrilled. He was convinced that the revolution had begun. "To arms, peasants and workers!" he wrote. "Hold secret meetings, form fighting units, get weapons wherever you can." He wrote to colleagues in Saint Petersburg: "Organize at once and everywhere fighting brigades among students, and particularly among workers. Let them arm themselves immediately with whatever

Soldiers fire on protesters on "Bloody Sunday" in Saint Petersburg. The massacre set off more protests throughout Russia.

As unrest spread across Russia in 1905, the Russian army dealt harshly with protesters.

weapons they can put their hands on—knives, revolvers, kerosene-soaked rags for setting fires. . . . Some can . . . assassinate a spy or blow up a police station. Others can attack a bank to expropriate funds [take money] for an insurrection." Excited, Lenin made plans to return to Saint Petersburg.

Uprisings continued throughout Russia. In Saint Petersburg and Moscow, workers formed soviets, or councils, to coordinate their efforts. In June sailors on the battleship *Prince Potemkin* mutinied (rebelled against their commanders) in the Black Sea. Widespread strikes paralyzed the country.

By October 1905, Czar Nicholas had realized he would have to give in to some of the people's demands. He agreed to create a constitution. He gave people freedom of speech and freedom of the press. Political parties—even revolutionary ones—were allowed to operate openly. Finally, Nicholas agreed to the establishment of a Duma, or parliament, made up of appointed and elected representatives. But he reserved the right to disband the Duma at any time and to make decisions without its approval.

Lenin reached Saint Petersburg in late November. About a month later, a massive workers' uprising broke out in Moscow. Again, soldiers put down the rebellion with bullets. Russia was in chaos.

"WORMS IN THE GRAVE OF REVOLUTION"

The creation of a Duma worried Lenin and some other revolutionaries. They feared that if the czar continued to make democratic reforms, workers would settle for slight improvements and would abandon the revolution. Most other Russians, however, were encouraged by the creation of a parliament. Only men of certain wealth and status in their communities were allowed to vote. But when elections took place in April 1906, the Constitutional Democrats, nicknamed the Cadets, won a clear majority in the voting. This party favored liberal reforms and a western European style of democracy.

Lenin scorned the Cadets, calling them "worms in the grave of revolution." He warned workers that the Cadets were nothing but capitalists. They would always side with the czar and the nobility against the workers, he said. He continued to ridicule the Mensheviks and anyone else who disagreed with him. Lenin believed that only the Bolsheviks—with himself at the helm—held the key to Russia's future.

In the early 1900s, many Russians remained loyal to the czar. In this painting, a crowd throws a suspected revolutionary off a bridge in Moscow.

Chapter **FIVE**

RUSSIAN ROULETTE

RUSSIA IN **1906** WAS A PRESSURE COOKER. CZAR Nicholas had created a Duma, but he had done so under political stress and was not truly interested in democratic reforms. Nicholas mistrusted the first Duma, and vice versa. Only three months after its members were seated, Nicholas disbanded the body and called for new elections. His secret police kept chasing revolutionaries.

For their part, the revolutionaries were still bent on overthrowing the czar. The Social Revolutionaries bombed government offices and murdered government officials. The Social Democrats continued stirring up the proletariat from both inside and outside Russia. Lenin left Russia in 1907 and settled in Finland, where he set up a base called the Bolshevik Center.

Although at first many Social Democrats had opposed the Duma, they decided the second time to run for seats. In this way, they hoped to gain power in the government and use it to push along their revolutionary agenda. They and other socialist groups were quite successful in the elections, winning a large block of seats in the second Duma. The czar was irritated, and he disbanded the second Duma in less than six months. He also changed the election laws, keeping more citizens from voting.

The third Duma, which held its first meeting in November 1907, was more to the czar's liking. It had fewer Cadets and fewer socialists and more pro-government, pro-czarist members. Although the nation was still splintered into countless hostile groups, political tension calmed down somewhat. The economy improved, industry grew, farmers enjoyed several good harvests, and many working people lost interest in revolutionary ideas.

STAYING THE COURSE

Vladimir Ilyich Lenin, of course, had lost no interest in revolution. From Finland he worked tirelessly to spread his message. Later in 1907, with the police on his tail, he moved his Bolshevik Center to Switzerland.

By this time, Lenin had attracted a new group of Bolshevik lieutenants, including Alexander Bogdanov, Lev Kamenev, Grigori Zinoviev, and Joseph Stalin. Lenin and the other Bolsheviks stuck fast to their extremist views. Some Bolshevik operatives robbed banks, arguing that capitalists had gained their money by exploiting workers and therefore revolutionaries had a right to take it back. In late 1908, again fearing police harassment, Lenin and other Bolshevik leaders moved their headquarters to Paris.

Lenin remained in Paris for three years, but he feared he was too far from Russia to keep control of the growing Bolshevik movement. So in June 1912, he and Krupskaya moved to Cracow in Galicia (modern-day Krakow, Poland), right on the Russian border.

THE GREAT WAR

In 1914 Europe erupted into war. The opposing forces were the Central Powers, led by Germany and Austria-Hungary, and the Allied Powers, led by France, Great Britain, and Russia. The conflict was called the Great War (later called World War I).

Compared to the other nations of Europe, Russia was not well prepared for war. Its factories could not produce enough machine guns, artillery, airplanes, and other equipment for the soldiers. Russia didn't have enough railroad lines to carry supplies, food, and troops to the battlefield. At the start of the war, Russia had 6.5 million soldiers—but it had only 4.6 million rifles.

Nevertheless, Russians were enthusiastic and patriotic at the beginning of the war. People set aside their unhappiness with the czar and committed themselves to the war effort. Men rushed to join the army.

SECRET AGENTS

T he Bolsheviks and other revolutionaries took great pains to keep their operations secret. They used disguises, forged identity papers, secret printing presses, secret codes, and smugglers to carry out their activities without police detection. But the czar's police were just as determined to undermine the revolutionaries. They cracked many of the secret codes and planted undercover agents in revolutionary groups. One seemingly devoted Bolshevik leader, Roman Malinovski, was actually an Okhrana spy. He and other police agents knew much of what the revolutionaries were planning and doing. The spies often tried to weaken the revolutionary movement by stirring up fights between various revolutionary groups.

Instead of strikes, workers held patriotic rallies in the streets of Moscow and Saint Petersburg. The government even changed the name of Saint Petersburg to Petrograd (Peter's City) because Saint Petersburg sounded "too German," and Germany was the enemy.

The revolutionaries were split in their attitudes about the war. Some of them abandoned their anticzarist activities and became very patriotic. Some joined the Russian army. But most revolutionaries saw the war as capitalism in action. They observed that while governments and their big-business supporters fought to expand their power, land, and wealth via warfare, the working people—most notably the soldiers on the battlefield—suffered and died. Instead of killing one another, the revolutionaries argued, working people should throw down their arms, join together, and fight the ruling classes. Lenin agreed with this argument, and he put forward a more radical one: he hoped that Russia would lose the war. He thought that a Russian defeat would lead more quickly to the end of czarism.

When the war started, Lenin and Krupskaya were still living in Galacia, which was part of the Austro-Hungarian Empire. Therefore, the couple was in enemy territory. They had to leave Galacia for their own safety. They settled once again in Switzerland, which did not take sides during the war.

The German government, meanwhile, noticed the unpatriotic attitudes of Lenin and some other revolutionaries. Secretly, Germany began financing some Russian revolutionaries—after all, their anticzarist efforts were useful to Germany's goal of defeating Russia. For a time, Germany secretly channeled large amounts of money to Lenin to promote his Bolshevik program.

FIGHTING ON ALL FRONTS

From the start, the war went badly for Russia. In battle after battle, the well-equipped Germans destroyed the struggling Russian army. Poorly fed and lacking equipment, Russia's troops suffered through the cold winter of 1914–1915. They soon lost their enthusiasm for battle. Thousands deserted (abandoned the army) or surrendered to enemy troops instead of fighting.

Inside Russia, people were equally discouraged. The defeats on the battlefield left them humiliated and angry with the government. Husbands, brothers, and sons were dying by the thousands. Then the economy began to suffer. Prices soared, especially food prices. The railroads were overloaded with military demands and could not deliver enough food from the countryside to the cities. Even when food was available, many workers could not afford to buy it.

Everyone—workers, peasants, students, revolutionaries, and nobles—blamed the czar. The Duma charged that he was mismanaging the war. But Nicholas dismissed their criticism. Instead, he decided to personally take command of the troops in battle. On September 4, 1915, Nicholas left for the front.

By then, the czar's wife, Czarina Alexandra, had fallen under the spell of Grigori Rasputin, a Russian holy man. The vulgar and unkempt Rasputin had many strange habits. Mysteriously, he was able to relieve the suffering of Alexis, the czar and czarina's son, who had a blood disorder called hemophilia. Thus Rasputin wormed his way into Alexandra's inner circle. With Nicholas away at the front, Alexandra began indirectly running the government. She was a die-hard autocrat who made no secret of her hatred for the Duma, democracy, and the common people. (In turn, most Russians disliked her, especially because she was German.)

The hardships of World War I were felt most keenly by Russian peasants, such as those pictured here.

With Rasputin's input, Alexandra wrote to Nicholas at the front, telling him to dismiss anyone who backed reform and to appoint only loyal czarists to government posts. The czar obeyed his wife, no matter how misguided her ideas. High government officials were hired and fired at a dizzying speed.

As the government stumbled, losses continued on the battlefield. More soldiers deserted. Some rebelled against their officers. Hungry, cold, and short on coal for heating, city-dwellers were no longer patriotic. Workers began to strike—refusing to work to protest shortages and their suffering. In the Duma, people of all political leanings called for Nicholas to abdicate (give up) the throne.

In 1917 Trotsky, right, *rejoined Lenin,* left, *to spearhead the revolution.*

Chapter **SIX**

REGIME CHANGE

IN **PETROGRAD IN LATE FEBRUARY 1917, PEOPLE'S**
frustrations finally reached the boiling point. Masses
of workers took to the streets. They demanded food,
an end to the war, and the czar's abdication. The
crowds swelled into the hundreds of thousands. Then
thousands upon thousands of soldiers joined the
rebellion, storming government buildings.

Nicholas was still at the front. When he learned that
protesters had taken Petrograd, his first instinct was
to send troops to put down the rebellion. But his generals saw the Petrograd rebellion as only the tip of the
iceberg. If the czar didn't step down, they warned, the
rebellion might spread to the frontline troops fighting
the Germans. Then the war would be lost.

After years of defiance, Nicholas finally followed the advice of his generals and top government officials. He abdicated on March 2. In his place, the Duma formed a provisional (temporary) government, led mostly by Cadets. At the same time, workers and soldiers hastily formed a body called the Petrograd Soviet. It took on some of the responsibilities of governing the nation. Meanwhile, Nicholas and his family retreated to their country home at Tsarkoe Selo, outside Petrograd, where they were placed under house arrest.

THE SEALED TRAIN

Back in Zurich, Lenin was eager to get to Petrograd to spearhead the long-awaited revolution. But almost all Europe was at war, and Lenin was a wanted man. If he traveled through a nation that was allied with Russia, he might be arrested for his revolutionary activities. If he traveled through a nation that was fighting against Russia, he might be killed or captured as an enemy agent.

Lenin worked out a plan. With Swiss officials acting as go-betweens, he asked the Germans to let him and a group of fellow revolutionaries travel safely through Germany by train. In exchange, Lenin promised to have the provisional government release an equal number of German prisoners from Russia.

German leaders were pleased with the proposal. They knew that Lenin and his Bolshevik faction opposed the war. They hoped Lenin would take over Russia and pull it out of the fighting.

So Lenin, Krupskaya, and thirty other Russian exiles, mostly Bolsheviks, departed Zurich on what came to be called the sealed train. The name implied that the Russians were completely sealed off from any Germans during the trip (and thus could not be accused of dealing with the enemy). The name was something of an exaggeration, because the revolutionaries did have contact with some Germans. In any event, the journey took them by train, then ferryboat, then train again, across Europe from Switzerland to Russia.

Arriving on April 3 at the Finland Station in Petrograd, Lenin wasn't sure what to expect. He hadn't set foot in Russia in ten years. He thought he might be arrested when he arrived. But his reception was anything but hostile. Crowds of workers and soldiers had flocked to the station to greet him. They carried red banners printed with revolutionary slogans. A military band played the "Marseillaise," a rousing song from the French Revolution (1789–1799). Soldiers and sailors lifted Lenin onto their shoulders and hoisted him on top of an armored car. Bathed in the blinding glare of searchlights, he addressed the crowd: "Long live the worldwide socialist revolution!" he shouted.

An Outline for Revolution

The next morning, Lenin addressed a group of Bolsheviks at Petrograd's Tauride Palace. He set forth a revolutionary program that came to be called the April Theses. In it, he called for Russia to end its war with

Germany. He denounced the provisional government as corrupt and bourgeois. He called for the creation of a citizen's army, the nationalization (state ownership) of all private land, and the creation of peasant-run farms. He said that all banks should be merged into one national bank and that workers and peasants should control government and the economy. And he urged his fellow Bolsheviks to act immediately to put these changes into place.

Other revolutionaries—the Mensheviks and the Social Revolutionaries—wanted to build on the existing Russian system to set up a socialist government. They wanted free and fair elections. They were willing to work peacefully with the provisional government to bring about a democratic, socialist state. By contrast, Lenin's April Theses called for the complete destruction of the current Russian political and economic systems. Lenin said that Russian society had to be destroyed and then rebuilt from scratch. And unlike the other socialist factions, Lenin and his Bolsheviks had no interest in creating a new society by democratic means. Instead, Lenin believed that society would be transformed by violence—by the workers seizing power from the capitalists. To this end, he created a military force called the Red Guards. It consisted of battalions of armed factory workers.

Moving in with his sister Anna and her husband, Lenin set about building up the Bolshevik ranks. He made speeches and wrote dozens of articles for

Pravda (Truth), the Bolshevik newspaper. He promised land to the peasants, bread and jobs to urban workers, and peace to everyone. He promised "All power to the Soviets"—the many informal workers' and soldiers' councils in operation around Russia. But he also planned to have his Bolsheviks take power within those soviets.

JULY DAYS

In May 1917, an old colleague joined Lenin in the Bolshevik camp. Leon Trotsky, a longtime Menshevik, had by then reconsidered his political stance and thrown in his lot with Lenin. Trotsky was a fiery speaker and a brilliant strategist. The two men made a smart and powerful team.

Meanwhile, working closely with the Petrograd Soviet, the provisional government tried to run the nation, despite severe inflation (rising prices), hunger, war, and political chaos. It promised to hold elections for a constituent assembly. This elected body would eventually take over running the government. It also vowed to continue fighting the war.

In late June, Alexander Kerensky, the new minister of war, hoped to rally Russians behind the war effort with a successful attack on German forces in Galicia. But the Russian attack stumbled. The Germans counterattacked and handed Russia another humiliating defeat. By then most Russians were thoroughly disgusted with the war—and also with the provisional

What Were the Soviets?

The soviets were loose organizations of workers, soldiers, or peasants. For instance, a factory with hundreds of workers might elect a small group of representatives to a soviet, or council. The soviet members acted as leaders and spokespeople for the workers in dealings with management and government officials. Elections were informal, conducted by a show of hands.

At first, factory workers formed soviets to coordinate their activities during strikes. Soon, groups of soldiers and peasants also formed soviets. Sometimes, several soviets grouped together to form city-wide or industry-wide soviets. In 1917 soviets from all around the nation sent delegates to the first and second All-Russian Congress of Soviets.

government, which seemed unable to solve their problems. More and more soldiers deserted their regiments. Whole units declared their loyalty to the antiwar Bolsheviks.

In early July in Petrograd, prodded by the Bolsheviks, people took to the streets once more. In what was called the July Days Uprising, sailors, soldiers, and workers swarmed through the city, shouting "Down with the government" and "All power to the Soviets." Carefully monitoring the mood of the people, Lenin and Trotsky thought the time might be right for a Bolshevik putsch, or takeover of the government.

But they changed their minds at the last minute, and the uprising petered out.

Then the provisional government struck a blow of its own. Armed with documents showing dealings between the Bolsheviks and the German government, Alexander Kerensky (by then head of the provisional government) accused Lenin of being a German agent—a traitor to Russia. Many Russians were appalled. Some people deserted the Bolsheviks. Government troops smashed the *Pravda* printing presses, and Kerensky issued arrest warrants for Lenin and other top Bolsheviks. Trotsky was arrested, but Lenin again proved slippery. He shaved off his beard, donned a wig and worker's clothing, and escaped to Finland.

"ASSUME POWER AT ONCE"

From his hideout in Finland, Lenin continued to direct Bolshevik activities. Using a team of secret messengers, he called for an armed uprising against the provisional government.

He also worked on a new book, initially called *Marxism and the State* but later published as *The State and Revolution*. In this book, Lenin described his vision of communism. In a communist society, he explained, ordinary workers would control every aspect of government. People would live in communes, or group households. The government would provide for everyone's needs, such as food, health care, and housing. There would be no private property. Government officials would be paid

This false passport allowed the disguised Lenin to escape to Finland after Kerensky issued a warrant for his arrest in 1917.

the same as factory workers. The people would serve as their own army, and all citizens would work for the state.

Back in Russia, the provisional government continued to struggle. It survived a coup (takeover) attempt by a military leader named Lavr Georgyevich Kornilov, but the incident left it further weakened. At the same time, the Bolsheviks once again grew powerful. As Lenin had hoped, Bolsheviks gained control of more and more local soviets and finally took over the Petrograd Soviet. Trotsky, by then released from prison, became chairman of the Petrograd Soviet.

Lenin thought the time was finally right for an armed uprising. "History will not forgive us if we do not assume power now," he wrote from Finland in mid-September. "Assume power at once in Moscow and in Petrograd." He warned, "Delay means death."

THE COUP

Still in disguise, Lenin returned to Petrograd on October 7. Within a few days, the Bolsheviks went into action. They armed thousands of followers. They had Red Guards and pro-Bolshevik military regiments standing by for orders. They won over new regiments to their side. The takeover was planned for October 24–26, during the Second All-Russian Congress of Soviets.

Kerensky also prepared for the coup attempt. He amassed a force of loyal troops outside Petrograd. He assigned other troops to protect the Winter Palace, headquarters of the provisional government. These soldiers included the Women's Death Battalion, a group of female soldiers sworn to fight to the death, and officer cadets (officers in training).

When the Congress of Soviets opened on the evening of October 24, the wheels of revolution were already in motion. Late that night, Bolshevik units arrested two government ministers. Bolshevik soldiers took over telephone exchanges, telegraph offices, banks, railroad stations, power stations, and bridges. Kerensky's forces were not strong enough to put up a fight.

Alarmed, Kerensky left the city on October 25 to

People flee fighting and death on the streets of Petrograd in October 1917. That month Bolshevik revolutionaries captured the Winter Palace and took control of the Russian government.

locate reinforcements. His remaining ministers were trapped inside the Winter Palace, with thousands of pro-Bolshevik troops in the streets and on ships in the harbor. The Women's Death Battalion and officer cadets were no match for the Bolshevik forces. The Bolsheviks began firing artillery at the palace, and the female troops quickly surrendered. Early in the morning of October 26, Red Guards rushed into the palace and arrested the ministers.

Back at the Congress of Soviets, Menshevik and Social Revolutionary delegates denounced the coup.

Trotsky scolded them in return. "You are a mere handful, miserable, bankrupt; your role is finished, and you may go where you belong—to the garbage heap of history," he shouted. Disgusted, the Mensheviks and other anti-Bolshevik factions left the congress, leaving the Bolsheviks to do as they pleased.

On the evening of October 26, Lenin addressed the congress. "We shall now proceed to construct the Socialist order," he said. He issued a Decree on Peace—calling for immediate peace negotiations between all nations fighting the Great War. Then he issued a Decree on Land—calling for the peasant takeover of all private land in Russia.

Finally, Bolshevik leaders announced the creation of a new provisional government, called the Soviet of People's Commissars (known by its Russian acronym, Sovnarkom). Lenin was the chairman, Trotsky was the people's commissar (official) for foreign affairs, and Joseph Stalin was the people's commissar for minority nationalities. All the commissars were Bolsheviks, although a few Left (radical) Social Revolutionaries allied themselves with the new government.

At last, after more than thirty years of tireless crusading, Lenin had achieved his dream. His Bolsheviks finally ruled Russia. But Lenin knew that to stay in power, he would have to work decisively and forcefully.

Red Guards stand watch over the entrance to Lenin and Trotsky's offices in Petrograd during the revolution.

Chapter **SEVEN**

THE NEW SOCIALIST ORDER

LENIN HAD A HUGE TASK ON HIS HANDS. HE HAD promised the people of Russia bread, peace, and land, and then he had to deliver. Weary of war, hunger, and revolution, some Russians looked hopefully to the new Bolshevik government to relieve their suffering. But many others were determined to bring down the Bolsheviks immediately. Almost as soon as Lenin and his group declared power, anti-Bolshevik armies began gathering outside Petrograd, in Moscow, and in other parts of the country. The Bolsheviks managed to keep control in the nation's two major cities, but elsewhere their power was limited.

From his offices in Petrograd's Smolny Institute, Lenin pressed forward with his plans for a new Russia.

He announced that banks, factories, and other big businesses would be nationalized. He decreed that laborers would have an eight-hour workday and would control their own workplaces through elected committees. He abolished all military ranks, declaring that all soldiers were equals. He announced free public schooling for all Russian children. He also drew up a temporary armistice, or truce, with Germany.

"WE ARE IN FAVOR OF FORCE"

But Lenin's efforts had a more sinister side. Soon after taking power, he created a secret police force. It was called the Extraordinary Commission for Combating Counter-Revolution, Speculation, and Sabotage. Known by its Russian initials, Cheka, the commission had broad powers. It could investigate, arrest, and punish anyone who was deemed to be a "counterrevolutionary"—that is, anyone who criticized or threatened the new Russian government.

Lenin announced that all Cadets were enemies of the people. He had their leaders arrested. Members of the "wealthy classes," including large landowners, investors, bankers, and other businesspeople, had to register with the government. Lenin also clamped down on the press. His agents seized printing presses and supplies of newsprint.

Even as Lenin tightened his grip on power, some people held out hope for a democratic Russia. Since the overthrow of Czar Nicholas earlier in the year, many

Russian people had called for a constituent assembly. In a show of fairness, Lenin decided to go forward with elections for assembly members. But when the results were tallied, the Bolsheviks had won only one-quarter of the votes. Lenin knew that he needed to shut down the assembly.

On January 5, 1918, when the newly elected assembly members gathered at the Tauride Palace in Petrograd, Lenin filled the meeting hall with soldiers. When members of opposing parties tried to speak, the soldiers jeered, booed, and pointed rifles at them. The Bolsheviks and their Left Social Revolutionary allies then labeled their opponents counterrevolutionaries. The Bolsheviks stormed out of the meeting and declared the assembly to be dissolved. Armed guards made sure that the opposing assembly members also left the building and never returned.

Two days later, the Bolsheviks opened the Third Congress of Soviets, with almost all Bolsheviks and Left Social Revolutionaries in attendance. With virtually no one to oppose them, the delegates declared that Sovnarkom was no longer a provisional government but was from then on Russia's permanent government. At the meeting, Lenin justified his use of intimidation. "Not a single problem of the class struggle has been resolved during the course of history except by force," he declared. "If force proceeds from the exploited working masses and against the exploiters—yes, then we are in favor of force!"

From War to War

On the war front, the truce with the Central Powers was shaky. Trotsky spent much of the winter months in Poland, negotiating a permanent peace treaty with the Germans. Called the Treaty of Brest-Litovsk, the agreement was signed on March 3, 1918. The treaty was a bad deal for Russia. In exchange for peace, Russia handed over about a quarter of its territory—including some of its most important farmland, railroads, factories, and mines, and more than one-third of its population.

Some Sovnarkom leaders fought to keep the deal from going through. The few Left Social Revolutionaries who had allied themselves with the Bolsheviks left the government in protest. But Lenin was determined to maintain power at any cost, even if that power extended over only part of the former Russian Empire. He also had a hunch that Germany was going to ultimately lose the war. If that happened, he knew, the Allies would void the treaty anyway.

Even as the treaty was being approved, Lenin worried that the deal might fall through and that German forces would advance on Petrograd and destroy the revolution. To be on the safe side, he and his fellow people's commissars moved their government to Moscow. They set up offices in the Kremlin, an ancient fortress. Lenin, his wife, and his sister Maria settled into a comfortable apartment on the first floor of the old Senate Building, one of many structures inside the Kremlin walls. Lenin's office contained about two thousand books, a portrait of Karl Marx, some simple furniture, and little else.

Soon after the move to Moscow, Lenin changed the name of the Bolsheviks to the Russian Communist Party. Russia itself became known as the Russian Soviet Federative Socialist Republic. The government and the Communist Party were one and the same. Lenin chaired both the state and the party. He ruled by decree, and his word was law.

Lenin continued to overhaul Russian society and the economy. He struck down the right of inheritance—meaning that parents could no longer pass down money and land to their children. Women were given equal rights with men. A great believer in the power of technology to change society, Lenin devised plans to build new electric power plants, power lines, and railroads across Russia. He continued to nationalize big businesses and tightened control over small ones. The government seized the homes, valuables, and even the clothing of the wealthy and gave them to the poor. In speeches and articles, Lenin boasted of the dawning of a new age in Russia. He predicted the transition "from the abyss of suffering and torture and hunger and barbarism to the shining future of Communist society, and the welfare of all, and enduring peace."

But Lenin's inspiring words were far from reality. The food shortages that had plagued Russia since the start of World War I worsened, particularly with the loss of so much farmland to the Germans. People in Petrograd had no bread. The government dealt with the crisis by seizing surplus grain from farmers and distributing it to city dwellers. Some peasants resisted or were simply unable to grow enough grain to satisfy the government. Lenin labeled them kulaks, or bourgeoisie farmers. He accused them of hoarding grain and selling it for their own profit. He ordered soldiers to seize their farms and in some cases to shoot the farmers on the spot.

The Germans were no longer a threat, but another war had already begun. Anticommunist armies were battling Lenin's forces in hot spots throughout Russia. These forces included former czarist officers and soldiers, socialists opposed to Lenin's policies, and ethnic fighters desiring independence. Lenin's soldiers, led by Trotsky, were called the Red Army. They labeled their opponents the Whites, or White Guard.

RED STANDS FOR REVOLUTION

As early as 1861, Russian revolutionaries flew red flags and banners. Lenin named his battalion of armed workers the Red Guards. They later became the Red Army. Why red? Revolutionaries have long fought their battles behind the color red. Rebels flew red banners during the French Revolution in 1792. The Bolsheviks labeled their opponents the Whites, or White Guards, after the counterrevolutionary forces of the French Revolution.

Lenin constantly warned Russians that if the revolution failed, czarism would return to Russia. The czar and his family were still in captivity, by then held at a house in the city of Tobolsk in Siberia. According to Trotsky, Lenin felt that "we should not leave the Whites a live banner to rally around." So Lenin had the entire royal family and several of their staff members murdered in July 1918.

Czar Nicholas II and his family (in foreground) *in Tobolsk, several months before Lenin had them murdered*

Dead Bolsheviks, flanked by enemy soldiers, lie in the snow during the Russian civil war.

Chapter **EIGHT**

BLOOD RED

BY THE SUMMER OF **1918,** LENIN AND HIS GOVERN-
ment had made many enemies. White Guards were
fighting his armies throughout Russia. Left Social Revolutionaries, formerly allies of Lenin's new government,
accused him of betraying the peasants with his grain
policies and destroying the nation with the Treaty of
Brest-Litovsk. The SRs resorted to their old tactics of terror and assassination to lash out at communist leaders.

In response, Lenin used his Cheka operatives to crack
down on the SRs. As with all his enemies, he labeled
them counterrevolutionaries, and he vowed to crush
them. Feliks Dzerzhinski, head of the Cheka, spoke
about the government's tactics at a press conference.
"We [the Cheka] exist on a basis of organized terror,

which is an absolutely essential element in revolution. We counter the enemies of the Soviet Government with terror and extirpate [wipe out] the criminals on the spot . . . the Cheka is obliged to defend the Revolution and crush the enemy, even if its sword sometimes chances to strike the heads of innocent people."

RED TERROR

On August 30, a young woman named Fanya Kaplan approached Lenin after he had made a speech to factory workers. She drew a revolver and shot him three times at point-blank range. Lenin was rushed to the Kremlin for medical treatment. Kaplan was arrested. She told the police that she had acted on her own and that she had shot Lenin for disbanding the constituent assembly. Kaplan was executed on September 3, and Lenin made a remarkable and quick recovery from his wounds.

In the fall of 1918, repression in Russia went from bad to worse. Since Kaplan had past ties to the Social Revolutionaries, the communists blamed the SRs for the assassination attempt. As Lenin was recovering, his staff ordered an increased level of terror against the SRs and other opponents. The Red Army newspaper announced: "Without mercy, without sparing, we will kill our enemies by the scores of hundreds, let them be thousands, let them drown in their own blood. For the blood of Lenin . . . let there be floods of blood of the bourgeoisie—more blood, as much as possible."

There followed a period of organized and widespread arrests, imprisonments, deportations, shoot-
ings, and hangings that came to be known as the Red
Terror. The government killed tens of thousands—
sometimes hundreds in one day. Lenin justified the

Citizens and Cheka officers surround bodies lying on a street in Petrograd. Such scenes were common during the Red Terror.

killings as necessary to the success of the revolution. Russia had to be cleansed of its enemies, he said. "The rule of capital will be extinguished only with the death of the *last* capitalist, the *last* landowner, priest, and army officer," explained *Pravda*.

SPIN

With the attempt on Lenin's life and his seemingly miraculous recovery, his followers began to speak of him in almost godlike terms. Prodded by the government, poets, authors, and artists all rushed to create images of him as the savior of Russia. Books and pamphlets offered fictionalized retellings of Lenin's life story. Writers asserted that Lenin's father had been a peasant, that Lenin's years outside Russia were marked by suffering and hunger, and other falsehoods.

This "Lenin cult" was part of a larger communist publicity machine. With it, the government attempted to paint a rosy picture of revolutionary society and to create support among the people for communist ideals.

The communists controlled information using censorship. Nothing could be published without the approval of the State Publishing House. All writings had to sing the praises of the new regime and promote the virtues of communism. "The business of literature must become a component . . . of Party work," explained Lenin. Many of Russia's most talented novelists left the country rather than submit to the new restrictions.

Painting, theater, films, and other creative works also had to support the party's goals. A government department called the Commissariat of Enlightenment oversaw all cultural activities. (Nadya Krupskaya served on the commissariat staff.) Much of the population, especially in the countryside, could not read or write. The communists spread their ideas via popular entertainments such as street theater and film. Troupes of actors visited factories, towns, and battlefields. They performed emotionally charged plays with stereotypical characters—the evil capitalist and the virtuous factory worker; the greedy landowner and the suffering peasant.

Posters, films, slogans, and even musical works served the same purpose. "Symphonies" were performed with motors, sirens, factory whistles, foghorns, and gunfire—the "instruments" of a new industrial, communist society. (Not surprisingly, many talented composers also left Russia during the early days of communism.) Trains and ships traveled to towns and military garrisons loaded with books, pamphlets, posters, and films that spread the message of the new regime. In every case, words and images showed the communist worker as heroic and engaged in a brave struggle with the evil forces of capitalism.

Schools, too, were used as "an instrument for the Communist transformation of society," according to one government document. In addition to learning the basics of language, math, and science, young people learned about the revolution, the communist form of government, and

This poster from 1918 celebrates "One Year of Proletarian Dictatorship." It shows happy, healthy workers standing over broken symbols of czarism (a shield and a crown). An abundant harvest and industrial growth occur under a rising sun.

ГОД
ПРОЛЄТАРСКОЙ
ДИКТАТУРЫ.
октябрь1917 - октябрь1918

Lenin's policies. At the university level, the government dismissed long-term professors and replaced them with loyal communists. Law and history classes were replaced with courses on Marxism-Leninism.

REALITY BEHIND THE ILLUSION

All the posters, plays, and films could not mask the reality of life in the early years of communism, however. The truth was that Russia's state-run economy nearly collapsed. Government planners and theorists had no experience running big businesses. New nationalized industries were able to produce only a fraction of what the same industries had produced under czarism. Harassed by military grain collectors, farming villages fell into chaos. Agricultural production plummeted. The tax system broke down, inflation soared, and government banknotes became essentially worthless. Making the situation worse, most foreign nations were wary of, if not hostile to, the new communist government in Russia and refused to buy its products.

In theory, a government agency called the Commissariat of Supply (Komprod) was in charge of distributing food and consumer goods to the population. Citizens received ration cards, which entitled them to a certain amount of meat, bread, coffee, salt, and other basics. Industrial workers received the largest rations. Members of the former bourgeoisie got the smallest. But the ration system was riddled with fraud and shortages. Even those entitled to the largest rations received only a few ounces of bread a day. Most people obtained what they needed through the black market—an underground network of illegal buying, selling, and trade.

The Commissariat of Labor assigned jobs to workers. All women worked outside the home, and children attended government-run schools or daycare centers. On "Communist Saturdays," everyone had to do extra, unpaid jobs, such as construction work or street cleaning.

Workers had been promised control of the workplace, but Lenin quickly abandoned this idea in favor of tight government control. Labor unions could no longer elect their own officials. Instead, the government appointed union leaders. And since all businesses were state owned or state controlled, workers who threatened to strike were labeled enemies of the state.

LENIN VERSUS GOD

L enin had long hated religion. As a teenager, he quit attending church and said he no longer believed in God. He and his fellow communists viewed religion as superstition and an obstacle to a modern, enlightened society. He viewed the church as a tool of the bourgeoisie. Lenin's family, like most Russians, belonged to the Russian Orthodox Church, a major Christian denomination. But the nation also had large communities of Catholics, Jews, and Muslims. Immediately after taking power, Lenin set about destroying organized religion in Russia.

His main target was the Orthodox Church, which had held great power under the czar. In a series of decrees, Lenin officially stripped the church of its power and privileges. He ordered the destruction or government takeover of church buildings and ceremonial objects. He outlawed the teaching of religion to children. He replaced religious holidays with communist festivals. His soldiers destroyed churches, monasteries, and relics (the remains of saints). Lenin also had thousands of priests and other church leaders arrested, imprisoned, and sometimes shot. The communists never officially outlawed religious worship, but they saw to it that the church became weak and obedient.

In Jewish communities, the government destroyed synagogues, banned Hebrew (the traditional language of Jews), and mocked religious holidays and rituals. Jews had long been massacred, harassed, and discriminated against under the czar. The new communist policies simply continued this longstanding mistreatment. The communists also harassed Catholics and Muslims.

The soviets still operated, but they were all under government control. Only communists were allowed to hold leadership positions.

A giant bureaucracy—or network of government officials—emerged to oversee the new economy and society. But the vast network only made the system slower and less efficient. And working inside every branch of government and every workplace was the Cheka, whose agents had swelled to 250,000 by 1920. In addition to its other terrorist duties, the Cheka ran the gulag—a vast network of prison camps, many of them in far northern Siberia. Inmates there were forced to labor under the most brutal conditions. In Lenin's time, thousands died of starvation, exposure, and overwork.

As a backdrop to the ongoing hunger, repression, and despair, the nation was still fighting a chaotic civil war. Its battle lines were constantly shifting. Control of territory went back and forth between the Reds and the Whites. Despite the shifts, the Reds always held Moscow, Petrograd, and most other big cities, as well as the communications and transportation lines in between. The Whites were scattered around the edges of Russia. It was difficult for White commanders in different areas to communicate and coordinate their actions with one another. This situation gave the Reds a distinct advantage through much of the war. In early 1920, the civil war finally ended with a Red victory. Historians estimate that some 13 million soldiers and civilians were killed during the conflict.

Lenin (center, on balcony) *addresses a crowd in Petrograd in July 1920.*

Chapter **NINE**

CHAOS AND CONTROL

BY **1920** THE RUSSIAN ECONOMY HAD REACHED ITS breaking point. The nation endured a drought and a bad harvest, reducing already low supplies of grain. People were desperate for food. By the thousands, they died of hunger and disease. As had happened many times in the past, peasants began to rebel. In Petrograd, workers threatened to strike and demanded freedom of the press and other civil rights. Soldiers and workers revolted at the Kronstadt naval base near Petrograd. Lenin responded as usual with terror and repression. Protesters were arrested, imprisoned, and sometimes executed on the spot. Their families, too, were subject to arrest and execution.

ABOUT FACE

But Lenin was forced to face facts. His economic policies were a failure. He had alternately blamed kulaks, White Guards, SRs, the church, capitalists, and other "counterrevolutionaries" for the suffering in Russia. But by early 1921, he had no one left to blame but himself. He had to change the nation's economic course. He did so with the New Economic Policy (NEP). This policy reintroduced capitalism to Russia on a limited scale. The government retained control over large industry, banking, wholesale and foreign trade, and transportation. But small stores and businesses were again allowed to operate freely. The government stopped taking grain from peasants. Lenin even approached foreign nations—those he had long denounced for their capitalist practices—to make new trade agreements.

Some fellow communists were shocked. Lenin appeared to be abandoning the communist principles that the revolutionaries had fought so long and hard to put into place. But Lenin dismissed the criticism. He said that by adopting some capitalist measures, he was merely taking advantage of the benefits of capitalism to strengthen communism. "The New Economic Policy," he assured skeptics, "has changed nothing radically in the social system of Soviet Russia, nor can it change anything so long as the power is in the hands of the workers." He continued, "I believe this capitalism is not dangerous to us."

The United States, Great Britain, and other western European nations were cautiously optimistic about Lenin's new policy. To them, Lenin appeared to be abandoning his "wild" theories of communism in favor of commonsense business practices. David Lloyd George, the British prime minister, remarked, "The moment [the Russians] begin to realize they cannot run their country except upon the same principles which have brought prosperity to other countries, they will begin to realize that the only way to bring prosperity to Russia is to put an end to their wild schemes."

NEP did help the economy slightly. Food production increased. But the improvements came too late for millions of Russians. By the spring of 1921, Russia was in the grip of a deadly famine. In some places, peasants resorted to eating grass, tree bark, rodents, and animal carcasses. Millions left their farms and villages in a fruitless search for food. In big cities, people died in the streets and were buried in mass graves. Disease attacked the weak and starving people. Epidemics of typhus, cholera, typhoid fever, and smallpox raged throughout the nation.

Lenin hated to ask the outside world—especially capitalist countries—for help. But the situation was desperate. He reluctantly allowed other leaders to seek foreign aid. The biggest help came from the American Relief Administration (ARA), headed by future U.S. president Herbert Hoover. The agency shipped food, medicine, and relief workers to Russia. By mid-1922, ARA was feeding 11 million Russians a day at soup kitchens. Deaths from starvation finally ended. Nevertheless, historians estimate that more than 5 million Russians died from starvation or disease between 1920 and 1922.

WITHERING AWAY

Lenin's fledgling government was still on shaky ground when he himself began to falter. He complained of headaches, nausea, fatigue, and insomnia. Used to working sixteen or seventeen hours a day, Lenin found that he could no longer put in a full day's work. A few years earlier, the government had given him a vacation home in the village of Gorki, about twenty miles from Moscow. He spent more and more time there but con-

Russian villagers form a funeral procession for victims of famine in 1921.

tinued with his duties as head of the Russian state.

On May 26, 1922, Lenin suffered a stroke. It left him temporarily paralyzed on his left side and unable to speak properly. The government called in doctors from around Russia and other parts of Europe. They did not all agree on a diagnosis. Some believed Lenin was suffering from advanced cerebral arteriosclerosis (hardening of the arteries of the brain). This potentially fatal condition had killed Lenin's father in 1886.

Lenin spent the summer resting at Gorki but returned to Moscow in October, determined to resume his normal workload. He continued his efforts to clean away the "earth's dirt"—his term for intellectuals, engineers, physicians, scientists, and other professionals who threatened his regime. As usual, these "enemies of the state" were punished with imprisonment, execution, and exile. In December 1922, all Russian-held territory was reorganized as the Union of Soviet Socialist Republics (USSR), or the Soviet Union.

Also in December, Lenin endured two more strokes. He sensed that he was going to die. His colleagues also knew the true extent of his illness—although it was kept a secret from the public. Throughout 1923, the government issued a series of upbeat reports. They said Lenin was simply suffering from exhaustion and was on his way to a full recovery.

But inside the Kremlin, the question loomed: Who would take the reins of government when Lenin died? The obvious choice was Joseph Stalin, who by then served as general secretary of the Communist Party's Central Committee. But Lenin had grown to distrust Stalin, whom he saw as rude and hot-headed. In secret, Lenin dictated his "Last Testament," stating that Stalin was not suited to lead the nation. Of all his colleagues, Lenin thought that Leon Trotsky was the most capable person to succeed him. Although Lenin tried to keep the testament a secret, Stalin found out about it. He was determined that the document should not stand in the way of his rise to power.

On March 9, 1923, Lenin suffered another major stroke. This time, his right side was completely paralyzed. He was unable to speak at all. He returned to Gorki, where his wife and sister Maria attended to him,

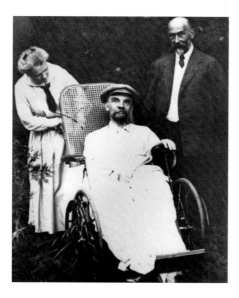

During the last few months of his life, Lenin was confined to a wheelchair.

assisted by nurses, doctors, and other staff members. Lenin's condition improved slightly. He regained his speech and managed to write with his left hand. He tried to remain involved in government activities, even visiting Moscow in October. But his health continued to fail. On January 21, 1924, Lenin fell into a coma. Later that evening, he died. He was fifty-three years old.

Lenin's death came as a shock to most of the nation, which had been kept in the dark about the severity of his illness. When people learned of the death, many broke down in sobs. Workplaces shut down, and factory sirens wailed. Everywhere people hung portraits of Lenin draped in black and red cloth. Lenin's body lay in state in Moscow's House of Soviets, in a grand hall hung with black banners, red ribbons, and chandeliers draped in black crepe. Between January 23 and January 26, more than half a million people filed past to view the body.

The elaborate funeral ceremony, held in Moscow's Red Square in below-freezing weather, was attended by tens of thousands. The funeral orator, Grigory Evdokimov, called Lenin "the world's greatest genius," "the bright star of mankind," and "the chief captain of our vessel." He declared that with his death, "from all ends of the earth there surge waves of lamentation, mourning, and grief." As the body was lowered into a temporary crypt, the entire Soviet nation came to a halt for five minutes. Factory sirens, train whistles, and ship foghorns sounded at full blast. All radio stations in the nation broadcast the same message: "Lenin has died—but Leninism lives!"

LENIN LIVES!

Lenin was not buried. His body was preserved with chemicals and placed in a glass coffin for all to see. The government built a special tomb to house the coffin and accomodate streams of visitors. Joseph Stalin succeeded in taking charge of the Soviet Union after Lenin's death. He saw the value of preserving Lenin—in both body and spirit—as a heroic symbol of the communist state.

The Lenin cult that had emerged after the 1918 assassination attempt soon grew to gigantic proportions.

LENIN'S BRAIN

Convinced that Lenin had been a genius, the Soviet government set up a special laboratory in which to study his brain after his death. Doctors removed the brain and cut it into thousands of small slices. Pressured by the government to make a favorable assessment, in 1936 Soviet scientists declared the brain to be exceptional. But in 1994, after the fall of the Soviet Union, scientists admitted that Lenin's brain was nothing out of the ordinary. The brain remains behind locked doors at the Moscow Brain Institute.

The Soviet government printed thousands upon thousands of medals, badges, banners, and posters bearing Lenin's image. It erected Lenin statues across the nation. Books, poems, songs, films, and folktales—usually packed with fictional details—told stories of Lenin's origins. In school and at Communist Party gatherings, young people learned about "Grandpa [Vladimir] Ilyich" and his devotion to children, workers, and peasants. Lenin museums, libraries, and reading rooms opened throughout the nation. The Communist Party announced the Lenin Enrollment Campaign to sign up new party members. Petrograd was renamed Leningrad. Lenin's hometown of Simbirsk was renamed Ulyanovsk. Lenin's birthday became a national holiday.

Indeed: Lenin had died—but Lenism lived on.

EPILOGUE: THE RISE AND FALL OF THE SOVIET UNION

After Lenin's death, Stalin took over as dictator of the Soviet Union. As bad as Lenin's Red Terror had been, Stalin's regime was many times worse. During his quarter-century in power, Stalin had millions of people killed or sent to gulags. No one was safe from his purges—not even loyal communists.

The Soviet Union and the United States were allies during World War II (1939–1945). But after the war, the two nations became bitter enemies. The United States watched with alarm as the Soviets spread their communist-style government to other nations around the world. Fearing one another, both the United States and the Soviet Union built up vast stockpiles of weapons. The rivalry between the two nations was called the Cold War (1945–1991).

But the Soviet government, for all its central planning and economic theories, could never successfully provide adequate food, consumer goods, or a decent standard of living for its people. In the 1980s, the Soviet people began to call for the end of communism. In 1991 the Soviet government broke apart. The Soviet Union was replaced by fifteen independent republics.

With the end of Soviet communism, Lenin finally fell from grace. In the former Soviet republics, people pulled down and destroyed Lenin statues. The Lenin Museum in Moscow shut down in 1993. Soviet historians, who had long been required to speak only good about Lenin, admitted that he was not a hero but instead was a ruthless and power-hungry dictator.

Winston Churchill, a twentieth-century prime minister of Great Britain, once wrote that Vladimir Lenin's birth was the worst misfortune that ever happened to the Russian people. Maxim Gorki, an acclaimed Russian writer and a Bolshevik, had warned during the revolution that Lenin would bring about "the downfall

Romanians celebrate the fall of communism by knocking down a statue of Lenin in Bucharest in 1990. Romania was a Soviet satellite state from 1948 to 1990.

of Russia. And the Russian people will pay for this in a sea of blood." Most historians would probably agree with these assessments. For all his talk of creating a "shining future" and "enduring peace," Vladimir Lenin spearheaded an era that brought only suffering, death, and deprivation to millions of people.

Even so, Lenin still has his backers. In the early twenty-first century, Leninists worldwide still meet, organize, and study his writings. His body remains on display in his tomb in Red Square, and millions of visitors come to view it each year. (Probably most go to see a famous, somewhat gruesome tourist attraction than to express devotion to Lenin.) Communist governments survive in a few countries, most notably China.

About one thing there is no debate: Vladimir Lenin changed the course of history in the twentieth century. He didn't do it alone. But one has to wonder, if there had been no Lenin, would there have been a Russian Revolution? A Soviet Union? Communist theory put into action? The Cold War? Chances are, if there had been no Vladimir Ilyich Lenin, the world would be a very different place.

SOURCES

7 Robert Service, *Lenin: A Biography* (Cambridge, MA: Belknap Press, 2000), 195.

8 Edmund Wilson, *To the Finland Station: A Study in the Writing and Acting of History* (New York: Farrar, Straus and Giroux, 1972), 533.

8 Ronald Clark, *Lenin: A Biography* (New York: Harper & Row, 1988), 191.

11 Rolf H. W. Theen, *Lenin: Genesis and Development of a Revolutionary* (Princeton, NJ: Princeton University Press, 1973), 34.

18 Leon Trotsky, *The Young Lenin* (Garden City, NY: Doubleday and Company, Inc., 1972), 41.

24 Theen, *Lenin*, 44.

26 Dmitri Volkogonov, *Lenin: A New Biography* (New York: Free Press, 1994), 19.

28 Robert Payne, *The Life and Death of Lenin* (New York: Simon and Schuster, 1964), 119.

31 Trotsky, *Young Lenin*, 204.

31 Ibid.

32 Clark, *Lenin*, 33.

32 Ibid., 35.

33 Louis Fischer, *The Life of Lenin* (New York: Harper & Row Publishers, 1964), 28.

40 Payne, *Life and Death*, 119.

45 Richard Pipes, *A Concise History of the Russian Revolution* (New York: Vintage Books, 1995), 106.

45 Clark, *Lenin*, 70.

48 Payne, *Life and Death*, 176.

50 Ibid., 184.

51 Ibid., 189.

51–52 Ibid., 189–190.

53 Ibid., 196.

65 Ibid., 313.

71 Ibid., 355.

71   Alan Moorehead, *The Russian Revolution* (New York: Harper and Brothers, 1958), 230.
73   Clark, *Lenin*, 274.
73   Moorehead, *Russian Revolution*, 252.
76   Clark, *Lenin*, 301.
79   Ibid., 307.
79   Payne, *Life and Death*, 456–457.
81   Ibid., 467.
83–84   Clark, *Lenin*, 370.
84   Pipes, *Concise History*, 224.
86   Payne, *Life and Death*, 493.
86   Volkogonov, *Lenin*, 362.
87   Pipes, *Concise History*, 324.
94   Clark, *Lenin*, 436.
95   Ibid., 443.
97   Nina Tumarkin, *Lenin Lives! The Lenin Cult in Soviet Russia* (Cambridge, MA: Harvard University Press, 1983), caption 4.
99   Ibid., 161.
100   Ibid., 162.
103–104   Payne, *Life and Death*, 408

SELECTED BIBLIOGRAPHY

Clark, Ronald. *Lenin: A Biography.* New York: Harper & Row, Publishers, 1988.

Figes, Orlando. *A People's Tragedy: The Russian Revolution 1891–1924.* New York: Penguin Books, 1996.

Fischer, Louis. *The Life of Lenin.* New York: Harper & Row Publishers, 1964.

Moorehead, Alan. *The Russian Revolution.* New York: Harper and Brothers, 1958.

Payne, Robert. *The Life and Death of Lenin.* New York: Simon and Schuster, 1964.

Pipes, Richard. *A Concise History of the Russian Revolution.* New York: Vintage Books, 1995.

———. *Russia under the Bolshevik Regime*. New York: Vintage Books, 1994.

Service, Robert. *Lenin: A Biography*. Cambridge, MA: Belknap Press, 2000.

Theen, Rolf H. W. *Lenin: Genesis and Development of a Revolutionary*. Princeton, NJ: Princeton University Press, 1973.

Trotsky, Leon. *My Life: An Attempt at an Autobiography*. New York: Pathfinder Press, 1970. First published 1930 by C. Scribner's sons.

———. *The Young Lenin*. Translated by Max Eastman. Garden City, NY: Doubleday and Company, Inc., 1972.

Tumarkin, Nina. *Lenin Lives! The Lenin Cult in Soviet Russia*. Cambridge, MA: Harvard University Press, 1983.

Volkogonov, Dmitri. *Lenin: A New Biography*. Translated and edited by Harold Shukman. New York: The Free Press, 1994.

Wilson, Edmund. *To the Finland Station: A Study in the Writing and Acting of History*. New York: Farrar, Straus and Giroux, 1972.

FURTHER READING AND VIEWING

BOOKS

Bjornlund, Britta. *The Russian Revolution*. San Diego: Blackbirch Press, 2005.

Gottfried, Ted. *The Road to Communism*. Minneapolis: Twenty-First Century Books, 2002.

Kort, Michael. *The Handbook of the Former Soviet Union*. Minneapolis: Twenty-First Century Books, 1997.

Marquez, Heron. *Russia in Pictures*. Minneapolis: Twenty-First Century Books, 2004.

Naden, Corinne, and Rose Blue. *Lenin*. San Diego: Lucent Books, 2003.

Streissguth, Thomas, ed. *The Rise of the Soviet Union.* San Diego: Greenhaven Press, 2001.

Vail, John. *"Peace, Land, Bread!": A History of the Russian Revolution.* New York: Facts on File, 1996.

Zuehlke, Jeffrey. *Joseph Stalin.* Minneapolis: Twenty-First Century Books, 2006.

DVDs

Battleship Potemkin. Los Angeles: Delta Entertainment Corporation, 2004.

Battleship Potemkin was one of many films by acclaimed Soviet filmmaker Sergei Eisenstein. In this silent classic, Eisenstein re-creates the famous 1905 uprising aboard the battleship *Prince Potemkin.* The original release date was 1925.

October (Ten Days That Shook the World). Chatsworth, CA: Image Entertainment, 1998.

This silent movie by Sergei Eisenstein, first released in 1927, re-creates the dramatic events of October 1917 in Russia. In typical Soviet fashion, the revolutionaries are shown as dedicated and heroic.

Strike. Chatsworth, CA: Image Entertainment, 2000.

This brilliant silent film from 1925 is another classic by Sergei Eisenstein. Set in czarist Russia, the film tells the story of striking workers in a Moscow factory.

INDEX

OTHER TITLES FROM TWENTY-FIRST CENTURY BOOKS AND BIOGRAPHY®:

ABOUT THE AUTHOR

Margaret J. Goldstein was born in Detroit and attended college at the University of Michigan. She is the author of many books for young readers. She lives in Santa Fe, New Mexico.

PHOTO ACKNOWLEDGMENTS

The images in this book are used with the permission of: © Getty Images, pp. 2, 6, 17, 42, 51, 52, 54, 62, 74, 81, 82, 92, 96, 103; © Mary Evans Picture Library, pp. 10, 35; © Hulton-Deutsch Collection/CORBIS, pp. 15, 70; © The Granger Collection, New York, pp. 20, 39; © Bettmann/CORBIS, pp. 29, 85; © Photo Collection Alexander Alland, Sr./CORBIS, p. 30; © Stock Montage/SuperStock, p. 36; Illustrated London News, p. 47; © Brown Brothers, pp. 61, 72; Library of Congress, p. 88 (LC-USZC4-5024); © Slava Katamidze Collection/Getty Images, p. 98.

Front cover: Library of Congress (LC-USZ62-101877). Back cover: © Hulton-Deutsch Collection/CORBIS.